Theme **A**uthor **G**enre **S**imilarity

Literarische Texte für den Englischunterrich
Herausgeber: Prof. Dr. Albert-R

DREW HAYDEN TAYLOR

TORONTO AT DREAMER'S ROCK

Herausgegeben von
Prof. Dr. Albert-Reiner Glaap

Cornelsen

Toronto at Dreamer's Rock

First published by Fifth House Publishers,
Saskatoon, Saskatchewan, Canada

Verlagsredaktion
Neil Porter

Technische Umsetzung
Jutta Debo

Umschlagbild
John Dunne, Magna Ashby, Leics.

www.cornelsen.de

1. Auflage, 4. Druck 2008

Alle Drucke dieser Auflage sind inhaltlich unverändert und
können im Unterricht nebeneinander verwendet werden.

Druck: Druckhaus Berlin-Mitte

ISBN 978-3-464-66574-9

Inhalt gedruckt auf säurefreiem Papier aus nachhaltiger Forstwirtschaft.

Contents

Abbreviations

abbr.	abbreviation	It.	Italian
adj.	adjective	jn.	jemanden
adv.	adverb	jm.	jemandem
AE	American English	n.	noun
BE	British English	o.s.	oneself
cf.	confer	pl.	plural
derog.	derogatory	pron.	pronunciation
e.g.	for example	sing.	singular
esp.	especially	sb.	someone
etc.	and so on	sl.	slang
fml.	formal	sth.	something
idm.	idiom	usu.	usually
infml.	informal	v.	verb

Drew Hayden Taylor and *Toronto at Dreamer's Rock*

It's always difficult to separate oneself from one's work and one's life, since for an artist they are usually intertwined on many levels. I am a product of my environment and my work is a product of me. Even though I have lived in the city for the past 13 years, all my stories and plays still take place on the Reserve, for that is the world I know best. It is the wellspring I draw from most, for it is the one that nourished me the best. And if nothing else, perhaps I can, through my work, open a window or two into that community for the rest of the world.

Who is Drew Hayden Taylor?

- *was born in 1962 to an Ojibway mother from Curve Lake First Nations Reserve, Ontario*
- *graduated from Seneca College with a diploma in Radio and Television Broadcasting*
- *successful career as a writer for stage and screen and writer and director of several documentary films*
- *has worked as a Native Affairs reporter for CBC Radio*
- *has written articles on Native arts and culture for several Canadian periodicals*
- ***Toronto at Dreamer's Rock** won the Chalmers Canadian Play Award in 1992 for the production by De-ba-jeh-mu-jig Theatre Group*
- ***The Bootlegger's Blues** won the Canadian Authors' Association Literary Award for Best Drama in 1992*
- *has written several short stories and plays*
- *teaches workshops in scriptwriting and playwriting*
- *has been Artistic Director of Native Earth Performing Arts since 1994*

2 **intertwine:** be twisted together to become joined 6 **wellspring:** source of a spring or stream · **draw sth. from sth. else:** take sth. (esp. liquid) from sth. else

For lack of a better term, I consider myself a contemporary storyteller. Like the traditional storytellers before me, I strive to tell stories that hopefully are multi-layered: they have a metaphoric level, a moral level, a historical level, an allegorical level, an entertaining level and so on. But I guess, in the long run, it is up to the reader or actor to decide if I have been successful.

I once had a conversation with a traditional storyteller talking about the importance of stories and I asked her about where somebody like me fit into the grand scheme of things. She smiled and said, quite wisely, "we need the new stories as much as we need the old ones."

Toronto at Dreamer's Rock is a very personal story to me. It is partially my story, and if I can be so bold, the story of many young Natives who are trying to find out who they are in this rapidly changing world. And I would guess, like many successful coming-of-age stories, the feelings and impressions it stirs reach outside of the Native community. Otherwise, I guess, there would be no interest in publishing it in Germany. I found in my many travels that people from all over the world can relate to Rusty's anger and confusion, for which of us hasn't found themselves trapped, in one way or another, between the ways of their grandparents and the new ways of life being offered today?

As a kid growing up on the Curve Lake Reserve in Central Ontario, Canada, I faced many such issues on a daily basis. But back then, I didn't know they were issues. Hearing my mother's language spoken was as natural as going swimming in the lakes. But the fact that I, for various reasons, never picked up that beautiful tongue, has haunted me to this very day. That and a million other little details of everyday Native life that define who we are and where we came from are rapidly disappearing. *Toronto at Dreamer's Rock* is my little way of showing how we must understand and respect the past before we can move into the future.

That is true of all cultures. That is one of the interesting things about this play; that in my naive and innocent blunderings into the world of theatre (for after all, this was my first play) I stumbled upon a culturally specific yet amazingly cross-cultural story.

2 **strive:** try hard 3 **multi-layered:** having many different levels 12 **bold:** brave and daring 15 **stir:** cause to be moved or touched 19 **trapped:** (here) having the feeling that one is caught between two things 25 **haunt sb.:** (of sth. unpleasant) return repeatedly to sb.'s mind 32 **blundering:** act of making silly mistakes 33 **stumble upon sth.:** come across sth. by chance

Originally many years ago, I was asked to submit a story idea to a theatre workshop for a Native Theatre company called De-Ba-Jeh-Mu-Kig Theatre Group. At the time, I was facing something of an identity crisis. I have light brown hair and bluish-green eyes, not the familiar dark looks of Canada's Native people. I have spent most of my life since leaving the Reserve convincing people that, though I am biologically half white, I was raised by my Ojibway mother on an Ojibway Reserve. Both Native and non-Native people have trouble believing that.

So, growing out of that continuing sense of frustration, I wanted to write something that explored what being "Native" meant to different people. Just as being "German" means different things to different people, so do "English", "French" and so on. It was from this idea that *Toronto at Dreamer's Rock* came: three different people, from different periods in time, with different perceptions of what being "Native" meant.

However, if they came from totally unrelated backgrounds, they would need some method of connecting with each other, something that would give them a common voice in order to interact. That is why Rusty, Keesic, and Michael are all 16. The older we get, the more diversified our interests become. However, a 16-year-old boy is a 16-year-old boy in any culture, and that is something we can all relate to.

Together the boys argue, laugh, joke, talk about girls, fight and philosophize. They question who each of the others are and in return are questioned themselves. 500 years are put up for inspection.

On a personal level, the success of *Toronto at Dreamer's Rock* surprises me, actually it astounds me. The original director of the play once told me, "it's such a wonderfully simple idea, people will say 'why didn't I think of that'". Perhaps that's part of its appeal. In the last five years *Toronto at Dreamer's Rock* has been produced eight times professionally, and half a dozen times by high schools across Canada. In several of the productions out west, I have let the directors change the aboriginal language to the local indigenous dialect, be it Cree or Coastal Salish, to make it more relevant to the audience they are serving.

1 **submit sth.:** give sth. for consideration 14 **perception:** view 19 **diversify:** vary 26 **astound sb.:** surprise sb. 32 **indigenous:** native

I have even been approached several times by various women who have said, basically, that *Toronto at Dreamer's Rock* is a great coming-of-age story for teenage boys, it would really be great if there was a companion piece for girls. A truly interesting thought (especially for a writer who believes a tale is never finished being told) but I can't help wondering if I, as a male writer, would have the right, or ability, to write a piece such as that. A female coming-of-age story is a very specific and personal concept, and while I have very strong and complete female characters in my other works, I have reservations about this particular idea. Perhaps this is for a woman to write.

That all said and done, I am delighted that Rusty, Michael and Keesic (and the Crow) are being introduced to Germany. I hope they will not have too much beer, sausages and french fries covered in mayonnaise. They are good boys, perhaps a little misdirected at times but essentially just and moral. Please take care of them.

Drew Hayden Taylor

May 1995

STORIES ARE MEMORIES
THAT MUST BE SHARED WITH THE UNIVERSE,
BECAUSE IF THEY AREN'T
THE UNIVERSE BECOMES A MUCH SMALLER PLACE.

To my mother,
who is still waiting for me
to get a real job

Production Notes

Toronto at Dreamer's Rock premiered on the Sheshegwaning Reserve, Manitoulin Island, Ontario, on 3 October, 1989; it was produced by De-Ba-Jeh-Mu-Jig Theatre Group, Wikwemikong Unceded Reserve, Manitoulin Island, under the direction of Larry Lewis.

Dreamer's Rock is a real place with real power. It is located beside a highway on the Birch Island Reserve, and many people still go there for guidance. Care should be taken in the depiction of such a sacred place.

Toronto at Dreamer's Rock was designed as theater-in-the-round. The set should be elevated to give the impression of height and so the cast can look over the audience into the distance. It should also be fairly small to give the impression of the top of a rock outcropping. With such a confined space, the action and interrelation of the characters is amplified. *Toronto at Dreamer's Rock* is a dialogue-oriented play with a limited amount of action, so this will help intensify the movement.

The language used during the opening and closing sections of the play is Odawa/Ojibway, the language indigenous to the area of Dreamer's Rock. The final paragraphs of the play have purposely been left ambiguous to allow the production company a chance to research and fashion their own closing prayer and song, depending on the area and the nation they belong to.

DREW HAYDEN TAYLOR

Toronto at Dreamer's Rock

Cast of Characters
(in order of appearance)

Rusty a boy from the present

Keesic a boy from the past

Michael a boy from the future

Location:
Dreamer's Rock, Whitefish River (Birch Island) Reserve, Ontario.

Time:
A relative term in this play, but it opens on a lazy Saturday afternoon during the summer of 1989.

The setting is the top of Dreamer's Rock, a large outcropping of rock overlooking a scenic valley. It is early evening and a gentle breeze blows across the Rock. RUSTY, *a 16-year-old boy, is making his long climb up the hill. He is listening to his Walkman, singing a heavy metal tune at the top of his lungs. At the summit at last, he turns off his Walkman, then walks over to a ledge. He puts one foot up on the ledge and leans on it, looking at the wondrous scenery.*

RUSTY: My home, my people, my beer store. *[He takes a bottle of Labatts Blue from his knapsack.]* As far as my eye can see … nothing but the little birds and me. *[Chuckles.]* For all it's worth.

He lifts the beer but before he can drink, he hears a crow cawing nearby. He stops, momentarily surprised.

Get your own, stupid crow. *[He looks around, shrugs, then holds up his beer in a mock salute.]* To Dreamer's Rock, the one place on Manitoulin you won't find beer bottles. *[He empties the bottle; the crow is cawing, but Rusty ignores it.]* Until now, that is.

Drumming begins, amid the cawing of the crow. RUSTY *begins to bounce on the rock, against his will.*

What the …?

Suddenly, he is on his feet, doing an elaborate and exhausting crow hop. This dance lasts for two full minutes. Finally, he collapses into the indentation in the rock, a place worn away by the generations of boys who have gone to the rock for their vision. He looks up at the sky, fighting for breath.

So blue, the sky. I wish I was up there. Speaking of Blue, I think it's time for another one.

1 **outcropping:** part of a rock which sticks out of the surface of the ground 2 **scenic** ['si:nɪk]: beautiful to look at 5 **summit:** top 6 **ledge:** part of a rock etc. which sticks out from a cliff 7 **wondrous:** wonderful 8–9 **Labatts Blue:** type of Canadian beer 10 **chuckle:** laugh quietly 11 **crow** [krəʊ]: Krähe · **caw** [kɔ:] (v.): make the sound of a crow 14 **mock:** imitated, not genuine 15 **Manitoulin:** Canadian island on Lake Huron 20 **elaborate:** very complicated · **exhausting:** demanding a lot of energy 22 **indentation:** Ausbuchtung

He reaches for another beer. The crow cries out.

Hit the road, crow. Fly, hit the sky. Can't you crows understand English? Then try some Indian. Kiss my geed, you stupid crow.

He jumps to a ledge on the rock. On another ledge, behind Rusty, Keesic *appears.*

Keesic: Kiss my geed? Nikiknendaan endaming ojiid, wagnen dash kina endman. [I know what a geed is, but what does the rest of it mean?]

Rusty *whirls around startled and finds himself looking at* Keesic, *a boy about his age.* Keesic *is dressed in a buckskin breech, identical to the kind worn several hundred years ago.* Rusty *doesn't know if this is a practical joke or something truly weird. He doesn't say anything for a moment as he slowly circles* Keesic, *trying to figure out what is going on.* Keesic *points at* Rusty*'s clothing with a puzzled expression.*

Zhaawshkwaande, wagnen waawaashkeshwi yaan eshaawshkwaandeg? [Blue? What kind of buckskin is blue?]

Keesic *reaches out to touch* Rusty.

Rusty: Hey man, you stay away from me!

Keesic *suddenly recognizes that things have changed. He checks out the surrounding area.*

Keesic: O'omaa, zhinaagwad chi-minaabdamaabaan, kaawiin shwiingego. Mitigoog nepaatshinoog. [This place, it looks like the Place of Dreams, yet it isn't. The trees are all wrong.]

He turns to Rusty *for help.*

Kaawiin naasaab ezhimkwendmaan. Kiin na, manidoo dazhazhebik? Kaawiin gdo-shinaagzisii manido? Aaniindi yaayaan? [It's not like I remember it. Are you a spirit of the Rock? You don't look like a spirit. Where am I?]

3 **geed** [dʒiːd] (Odawa): bottom 8 **startled:** surprised 9 **buckskin:** made of soft leather (from male deer skin) · **breech:** pair of trousers 11 **practical joke:** trick played on sb. · **weird** [wɪrd; BE wɪəd] strange

RUSTY: This is wild. *[Looks at beer.]* What are they putting in this stuff these days?

KEESIC: Kaawiin gnistotoosnoon. Gnoonshin enweyang. [I don't understand you. Speak in our language.]

RUSTY: That sounds like Indian. English, man. Talk to me in English. Where did you come from? What's with the get-up?

As he says this, RUSTY *reaches up to touch* KEESIC*'s sleeve, but the moment contact is made, the magic happens.* KEESIC *and* RUSTY *are thrown to the ground, they roll and come up on their knees, stunned and surprised.* KEESIC *shakes his head clear, then looks at his sleeve where* RUSTY *touched him, then back at* RUSTY.

KEESIC: What did you do to me? What are you doing on this sacred site?

KEESIC *has barely finished the sentences when he realizes that he has changed languages. His face registers the shock.* RUSTY *is oblivious to* KEESIC*'s predicament, only aware of his own.*

RUSTY: Hey buddy, that was a nasty fall you took there. You okay?

KEESIC *jerks his head up at* RUSTY*'s voice, totally amazed but still confused.*

KEESIC: I understand …

KEESIC *grabs his own throat, terrified at the words coming out. Timidly he tries again.*

KEESIC: This is not my language …

KEESIC *freezes again.* RUSTY, *by this point, is beginning to get concerned.*

6 **get-up** (sl.): clothes 14 **oblivious to sth.:** not aware of sth. 15 **predicament:** unpleasant situation 24 **concerned:** worried

RUSTY: Hey, you don't look so hot. Geez, don't get sick on me, people probably wouldn't like it if you threw up on Dreamer's Rock, bad for tourists.

KEESIC, *not believing or understanding the new language he is speaking, grabs his throat and struggles to talk his own language, but he has forgotten it.* RUSTY *misinterprets the action as choking and quickly pulls out a beer and gives it to* KEESIC *to drink.*

RUSTY: Here, drink this.

KEESIC: Is it water?

RUSTY: To my family it is. They'd shower in it if they could.

KEESIC *comes close to* RUSTY, *and notices an aroma on* RUSTY'*s breath.*

KEESIC: Whatever it is, it makes you smell.

RUSTY: What are you, a critic? You try climbing up this rock carrying a couple bottles and see how you smell.

KEESIC: It's not sweat I smell, something deeper.

RUSTY: Hey, don't knock it till you've tried it. Here. *[Handing bottle to* KEESIC.*]* Take a swig.

KEESIC *is hesitant to take it.*

What are you, a wimp?

KEESIC *takes a big gulp. His face quickly registers distaste as he spits it out, handing the bottle back to* RUSTY *quite quickly.* RUSTY *is chuckling to himself.*

Funny, that's exactly how I reacted to my first sip.

1 **not look so hot** (sl.): not look well 2 **throw up:** vomit 6 **choke** (v.): have difficulty breathing 16 **don't knock it till you've tried it** (idiom): don't criticize it until you've tried it 17 **swig:** mouthful of a drink 19 **wimp:** weak person

KEESIC: That is horrible, like the water in a swamp.

RUSTY *smells his beer, shrugs, then takes a drink.*

RUSTY: I guess it is an acquired taste. Be happy you're not trying a 50, that stuff will rot out your sinuses.

KEESIC: You prefer that ... that ... liquid over water?

RUSTY: I've never brushed my teeth in it but yeah, I like it.

KEESIC *reaches over and touches* RUSTY's *denim jacket with wonder.*

KEESIC: And this? What animal does this skin come from?

RUSTY: *[Shrugging.]* It's a Levi.

KEESIC: It looks like all one skin. This Levi must be a big animal. I am called Keesic.

RUSTY: Keesic, eh? Your parents were born-again Indians, too, huh? My middle name is Mukwa. That means bear.

KEESIC: You must be a strong person to carry such a strong name.

RUSTY: *[Proudly.]* Can bench 110 pounds.

KEESIC: Bench? Pounds? You pound benches 110 times?

RUSTY: *[Getting tired of the charade.]* Get out of town. Look, I was here first. I came up here to be alone for a while, if you don't mind.

KEESIC: This is the Place of Dreams, you can never be alone here.

1 **swamp** [swɒmp]: wet, soft land 3 **50:** brand of strong Canadian beer 4 **sinus** ['saɪnəs] (pl. -es): Stirn- oder Nebenhöhle 15 **bench**: (v.) lift weights while lying on one's back; (n.) long wooden seat 15–16 **pound:** (n.) measurement of weight; (v.) smash

RUSTY: Well, not with people like you around, that's for sure. And what's with the fortune-cookie talk? You eat in a lot of Chinese restaurants or something?

RUSTY *turns away and walks a bit, hoping* KEESIC *will take the hint and disappear. Instead,* KEESIC *seems to be thinking.*

KEESIC: It's been a while since I have eaten, but I don't think I've ever hunted a *[Struggling with the word.]* Chinese restaurant.

RUSTY: Very funny.

KEESIC: It is summer now. *[He looks around.]* I've just spent the last three days fighting the wind and the snow to get here. And only to be met by summer. Why?

RUSTY: Maybe to wear one of those white jackets with the long arms that wrap right around …

KEESIC: Mukwa, do you know why …

RUSTY *answers quickly and harshly.*

RUSTY: Mukwa? Hold it right there, Tonto, people call me Rusty around here. And don't tell anybody I told you my middle name. It's embarrassing.

KEESIC: Rusty? What kind of name is Rusty?

RUSTY: *[Confused.]* What do you mean what kind of name? It's a name, my name. You got a problem with it, buddy?

KEESIC: No, it's just that I have never heard of anything or anyone called a "Rusty".

RUSTY: When I was young, my hair was kinda red, sort of a rust color, so I got called Rusty. Happy?

2 **fortune-cookie:** small biscuit containing a paper with a proverb (usually served in Chinese restaurants) 16 **Tonto:** Lone Ranger's Indian friend in the TV series "The Lone Ranger"

KEESIC: But what is a rust?

RUSTY: You've been out in the woods too long. Rust, you know, when metal gets old and wet, it turns rusty and falls apart. It, like, decays, I guess is the right word.

KEESIC: Metal?

RUSTY: You're really playing this to the hilt, aren't you? Metal, like bendable rock.

KEESIC *wanders away for a moment, perplexed, then turns to* RUSTY.

KEESIC: You were named after rotting rocks?

RUSTY: *[Insulted.]* My rocks ain't rotten. It's just a nickname. It don't mean anything.

KEESIC: But what power does a name have if it doesn't have a purpose or meaning?

RUSTY, *thinking his name is being insulted again, begins to get angry.*

RUSTY: Okay, I've had enough of this. If you don't like my name then just say it to my face then. Well, you got something to say?

KEESIC: *[Backing off.]* No, it's your name. I'm sure it's a fine name. Rusty.

RUSTY: Yeah, well watch it next time.

KEESIC: *[To himself.]* Strange people, what happened to the naming, in this strange place? I don't know where I am.

RUSTY: It ain't Kansas.

KEESIC: I must know, is this the Place of Dreams?

3 **decay** (v.): become old and rotten 6 **play sth. to the hilt** (idiom): not know when to stop
17 **back off:** move backwards 22 **It ain't Kansas:** allusion to the film *The Wizard of Oz*, when the heroine Dorothy realises she is no longer in Kansas but in a fantasy land

RUSTY: Of course, it's Dreamer's Rock. Everybody knows that.

KEESIC: Dreamer's Rock? I must be in the Land of Spirits. But why would the Great Spirit bring me here?

RUSTY: What are you talking about?

KEESIC: *[Ignoring* RUSTY, *thinking.]* The last thing I remember, before seeing you, was climbing up this place you call Dreamer's Rock. The rock was coated with snow and ice. My fingers bled from holding on, but I was finally here.

Rusty is waiting to hear the rest of the story.

RUSTY: And?

KEESIC: And what?

RUSTY: What happened next?

KEESIC: *[Shrugging.]* I slipped.

RUSTY: You slipped!

KEESIC: The rock was covered with ice … I went head over foot to the bottom and ended up here.

RUSTY: *[Not believing.]* At the top?

KEESIC: *[Rubs his head painfully.]* Some time the Creator works in mysterious ways.

RUSTY: I guess so.

KEESIC: *[Pointing.]* That mountain. That was never here.

RUSTY: *[Looking.]* That ain't no mountain, it's a cement factory.

KEESIC: Cement factory? What's that?

By this point, RUSTY *is beginning to get a little exasperated.*

RUSTY: It's a place that makes cement, you idiot.

KEESIC: Cement?

RUSTY: Yeah, like man-made rock, you know.

KEESIC: Why would man want to make rock? *[Gestures toward the landscape.]* There's rock as far as the eye can see.

RUSTY: Yeah, but you can shape cement.

KEESIC: Into what?

RUSTY: Well … a floor to stand on.

KEESIC: Like this? *[Points to the ground.]* This already has a floor of rock.

RUSTY: *[Getting frustrated.]* It's movable. You can put it places where there isn't a surface like this.

KEESIC: Then this cement is lighter than rock?

RUSTY: No!

KEESIC: Then why …?

RUSTY: *[Yelling.]* Never mind!

KEESIC *reacts to* RUSTY'S *frustration by backing up a bit.*

KEESIC: Not so loud. You'd think I was down by the lake the way you yelled at me.

RUSTY: Okay, I'm sorry.

1 **exasperated:** angry; frustrated

KEESIC: And those lines over there *[Pointing.]* cutting through the forest. What do you call them?

RUSTY: *[Looking.]* Oh. Those are roads.

KEESIC: Roads. And what do these roads do?

RUSTY: People drive on them. What else would you do with them?

KEESIC: I can't tell from here, what do they look like?

RUSTY: Roads? They are like very wide, hard paths, I guess.

KEESIC: Paths? That big? Hunting must be good to make people fat enough to need a path that wide. I have this picture in my mind of these roads bringing all these fat young boys here for their dreams.

RUSTY: You're talking about dream quests, aren't you? They don't do that much any more, it sort of died out about a hundred years ago I think. Occasionally you hear of some crazy fool trying it, usually the kid of one of those fool drummer types, but not much.

KEESIC *looks startled, and a bit stunned.*

KEESIC: No more dreams, no more visions, no fasting? Why?

RUSTY: I don't know. They just don't. None of my friends seem to want to sit out in the bush and starve for a week. Cuts into their social life.

KEESIC *kneels down at a particular spot, gently touching it, like he's remembering something. His voice takes on a gentle tone.* RUSTY *is intrigued by* KEESIC. *He's being drawn into his power.*

KEESIC: I think I am beginning to understand now. My visit to the Place of Dreams took place long before your time.

11 **quest:** search 15 **stunned:** shocked 21 **be intrigued by sb.:** be fascinated by sb. · **be drawn into sth.:** be pulled into sth. against one's will

RUSTY: Who are you? Rip Van McGregor? You can't be much older than me.

KEESIC: I believe I am 16 winters old.

RUSTY: I thought so. It's hard to pull something over on me when I've only had a couple beer.

KEESIC: But I am 16 winters when there are no roads or strange man-made mountains.

RUSTY: *[Disbelieving.]* Uh huh. Sure you were.

KEESIC: My vision told me nothing of this, any of this.

RUSTY: Your vision? You had a vision here? I don't remember hearing anything about that, and my mother's the biggest gossip around. She knows everything that goes on in the village.

KEESIC: I was here for five days with nothing but wind and the sun for companionship. I drank water, I chanted, I prayed for my vision to appear. Finally, one dark and windy night, it came. And went.

RUSTY: So that's how you got to be this crazy. No wonder. You were probably hallucinating or something with no food in five days.

KEESIC: The Creator told me how to live in images and stories that took time to figure out. But that is the way of the Creator. All things worth having must be earned.

RUSTY: So why are you up here again? Looking for DreamQuest, the sequel?

KEESIC: *[Not listening.]* My vision told me that I am to follow the path of medicine.

1 **Rip Van McGregor:** reference to Rip Van Winkle, the hero of Washington Irving's short story of the same name, who fell asleep and woke up 200 years later; McGregor is a popular surname in the Reserve on Manitoulin Island 4 **pull sth. over on sb.** (sl.): lie to sb. 11 **gossip** (n.): person who likes to talk about other people 22 **sequel:** the second part of sth.

RUSTY: And the problem is?

KEESIC: Sadly. I can't do it. I'm not strong enough. I'm afraid I will embarrass my family and people if I fail.

RUSTY: Bad scene. So if all your troubles started here, why come back?

KEESIC: This place helped me once. I was hoping it could do it again. Even in winter this place called out to me, and I came. And here I sit now. With you.

RUSTY: In the land of roads and cement factories.

KEESIC: Yes, strange, is it not?

RUSTY *is silent before he gives a short chuckle.*

RUSTY: And in this so-called vision of yours, there were no little white people running around telling you to go home and stay out of trouble?

KEESIC: White people? Is that what was in your vision?

RUSTY: I hate to bust your metaphysical bubble there, Moses, but I came here to drink. That's it in a nutshell. *[Turns to grab his beer.]* Speaking of nuts …

MICHAEL, *dressed in unidentifiable futuristic garb, stands on the rock, staring at* KEESIC *and* RUSTY.

MICHAEL: I don't believe this.

KEESIC *and* RUSTY *scream aloud, and freeze in their tracks.*

KEESIC: Yiiii!

RUSTY: Holy …

15 **bust** (v.): break, destroy sth. 16 **in a nutshell:** in a few words 18 **garb:** clothes

MICHAEL: They sound authentic.

MICHAEL *walks up to them and examines them closely, beginning with* KEESIC.

Pre-contact, no doubt. I'd say late woodland period. *[Touching* RUSTY*'s jacket.]* Standard outfitting for the 20th-century aboriginal. Denim. Once referred to as "jean".

KEESIC: *[Feeling* MICHAEL*'s sleeve.]* Another strange animal.

MICHAEL: *[Almost distastefully.]* Not animal, synthetic.

RUSTY: Where are you people coming from?

KEESIC: I am called Keesic, strange one. Are you from this time, too?

MICHAEL: Do I look like it?

KEESIC: No. You look funny. Funnier than this one.

MICHAEL: Where I come from, today is the first of May, 2095. *[He sees something in the distance.]* That, that's an *[Struggling with the word.]* automobile, isn't it? Almost looks like a '93 Eclipse.

RUSTY: A '93 what?

MICHAEL: I'm being rude. *[To* KEESIC*, enunciating very clearly.]* I am Michael. *[Touching his heart with his fist. He turns to* RUSTY*, extending his hand.]* I believe the contemporary greeting is "I'm pleased to meet you, and you might be?"

RUSTY: *[Voice cracking.]* Rusty.

The name seems to have struck a chord. MICHAEL *studies* RUSTY*'s face.*

RUSTY: What are you lookin' at?

4 **pre-contact:** from the period before the Europeans came 5 **aboriginal:** native

MICHAEL: Rusty what?

RUSTY: Just Rusty to you, pal. Why?

MICHAEL: You look very familiar.

RUSTY: *[Snickers.]* Maybe you're my great-great-great grandson. That's a laugh.

MICHAEL: I know your face from somewhere, and your name. Rusty! Rusty!

RUSTY: So if you're from the future, I'd have to be famous for a hundred years or something for you to know me. *[It dawns on him.]* Famous! Am I famous, huh, am I? What did I do? Am I a movie star or something? A rock star? *[He stops.]* What am I saying? My God, it's contagious. I'm crazy, too.

KEESIC: You are from this one's future?

MICHAEL: I didn't think it was possible.

KEESIC: All things are possible here.

This is too much for RUSTY. *He starts backing up and almost falls off the rock. He looks at the others as if they are crazy.*

RUSTY: What is this? You guys travel in pairs or something? Who are you?

MICHAEL: Philosophically, psychologically, economically, culturally? Be specific.

RUSTY: *[Yelling.]* Who the hell are you?

MICHAEL: You look upset.

4 **snicker:** giggle disrespectfully 12 **contagious** [kən'teɪdʒəs]: (of a disease) spreading by contact

KEESIC: He yells a lot.

RUSTY: *[Turns to* KEESIC.*]* You shut up, I still haven't figured you out yet. Look, I don't know where you guys are coming from, but I want you to go back there now. I mean it.

Michael turns to KEESIC, *ignoring* RUSTY.

MICHAEL: This is interesting. Judging by the material and stitching pattern, I'd hazard a guess of approximately 500 years ago my time. I knew it was pre-contact.

KEESIC: Pre-contact.

RUSTY *throws his hands up in frustration and turns away.*

RUSTY: And he still has all his teeth.

MICHAEL: It means you were here before the white man was, totally untouched, pure. I have a history teacher that would love a chance to interview subject matter like you. Both of you, actually.

RUSTY *steps in between the two, separating them, and then turns to* MICHAEL.

RUSTY: Wait a minute, just wait a minute, Flash Gordon, I'm tired of having my leg pulled. It's probably halfway down the hill by now. And I don't buy this time thing either. For the last time, who are you? Buckskin Bill here won't give me a straight answer. You got one? Is this a regular thing with you guys, or what?

MICHAEL *walks around* RUSTY *and looks off in the distance, taking a deep breath.* KEESIC *looks puzzled.*

KEESIC: How do you manage to hunt and feed your family when you talk so much and so loudly?

6–7 **stitching pattern:** Stickmuster 7 **hazard sth.:** suggest sth. 17 **Flash Gordon:** American science-fiction comic hero of the 1930s 18 **pull sb.'s leg:** lie to sb. for a joke 19 **buy sth.** (sl.): accept sth. as being true

RUSTY: I think I'm getting one of my mother's headaches. I never should have come up here.

KEESIC: I've been to the Place of Dreams many times, but never like this. Michael, I am called Keesic. Welcome.

MICHAEL: *[Animated.]* I have this pet theory about this particular spot.

RUSTY *makes a rude noise.*

Of course, I'm the only one who believes it, but I think it's true. Over those thousands of years that boys had their vision quests here, this area amassed a tremendous reservoir of power. And probably in the time between the two of you this power has gone largely unused. It's a type of emotional power, similar to the Poltergeist phenomenon common in Germany, and Rusty must have triggered it somehow! This is a pretty powerful place, Rusty, even in my time.

RUSTY: I don't care about this place, I just want to find out where you people are popping out of and why. Who's next, the ghost of Christmas present?

MICHAEL *bursts out laughing, but* KEESIC *doesn't understand it.*

MICHAEL: Don't worry, Rusty, I'm fairly certain I'm not a ghost. How about you, Keesic?

But KEESIC *has no idea what is going on.*

KEESIC: Ghost? What?

RUSTY: This is one of those days I should have gotten up, eaten my Rice Crispies, and gone right back to bed again. Look guys, I just wanted a nice quiet beer, and I didn't even get that with that damn crow bugging the hell out of me.

5 **pet theory:** favourite theory 15 **pop out of sth.:** come from sth. 15–16 **ghost of Christmas present:** one of the ghosts who appears to Scrooge, a character in Charles Dickens' novel *A Christmas Carol* 25 **bug the hell out of sb.** (sl.): drive sb. crazy

Suddenly RUSTY *has* KEESIC*'s complete attention.*

KEESIC: Crow?! Did you say you heard a crow? What did it say?

RUSTY: Caw. What else does a crow say? It just screeched a few times when I drank my beer, then it went away. *[Keesic looks worried.]* Why? What does a crow have to do with anything?

KEESIC: I don't know. But you know what a crow is.

MICHAEL *and* RUSTY, *confused, look at each other.*

RUSTY: *[Bluffing.]* Yeah, of course I do, but you better explain it to Michael anyways.

KEESIC: They are the messengers of the Creator and other powerful beings. If that crow was talking to you, it must have been for a reason. You should learn to listen, Rusty, it might have been trying to tell you something important.

RUSTY: Like where the garbage dump is.

MICHAEL: Messengers of the Creator! How quaint!

RUSTY: Forget the stupid crow. If everything you two are telling me is true, then why me, why you, why here, why now? *[Pause.]* I don't believe this. And why am I still talking to you? My mother warned me about people like you but she said they all lived in Toronto.

KEESIC: Toronto?!

RUSTY: You know about Toronto? Then you aren't real.

KEESIC: I'm as real as you are. My people are great traders. We make trips to the south for goods. And in trade it is better to understand the language of the people you are dealing with. Those people to the south have a word for where people gather to trade, but it covers any place where important things happen. It's called "Toronto".

14 **garbage dump:** place where rubbish is put 15 **quaint:** beautiful, but old-fashioned

RUSTY: So we're like a little mini-Toronto right up here. That's cool.

MICHAEL: Actually in my time, the metropolis of Toronto almost reaches to the shore of Huron. Traders, eh? What nation are you, anyways?

KEESIC *looks perplexed.*

KEESIC: We are the people.

MICHAEL: Did other nations have a name for you?

KEESIC: We are known by some tribes as Odawa.

RUSTY*'s ears perk up at that word.*

RUSTY: Hey, wow. I'm half Odawa. This is bizarre.

KEESIC: Half Odawa? What is your other half?

RUSTY: Ojibway, and I think there's supposed to be some Pottawatami floating around in my blood somewhere, too.

MICHAEL: Genealogically, I am mostly Odawa.

KEESIC: Ojibway? They live far to the northwest. And the Pottawatami don't live near here. How does their blood flow in your veins?

RUSTY: It's the Three Fires.

KEESIC: I don't understand.

RUSTY: You don't understand the Three Fires? What kind of Indian are you anyways?

MICHAEL: *[Stepping between them.]* A lot of nations were displaced by the coming of the whiteman. And, as a result, traditional migratory

14 **genealogical:** referring to family origin 22 **migratory:** having the habit of moving from one place to another to find food

patterns were disrupted. Eventually, the Ojibway, Odawa, and Pottawatami reached an agreement whereby they would share Manitoulin Island.

KEESIC: That's the third time you've mentioned this white man. Why is he white? Is he not well?

RUSTY: Well, that's a judgment call.

MICHAEL: I guess you could say he is another nation far to the east in your time. And in time, he came to this island here.

KEESIC: I have heard stories about these people. But I thought they were just stories.

MICHAEL *shakes his head confidently.*

MICHAEL: Well, they're coming. Taking an educated guess, I would estimate you to be from approximately the 1590s. And Champlain landed in this area around 1615. We're talking a couple of decades at the most.

RUSTY: *[Laughing.]* Boy, do you have a surprise coming. Guess who's coming to dinner? You better put out an extra 250 million plates, but be sure and check the silverware after.

Even MICHAEL *laughs at that one. But* KEESIC *remains in the dark.* MICHAEL *picks up* RUSTY*'s bottle of beer and examines it as if it were an interesting museum piece.*

MICHAEL: Labatts Blue! I didn't know they made this way back then … I mean now.

KEESIC: I don't like it.

1 **disrupt sth.:** break sth. up, disturb sth. 6 **judgment call:** question of opinion 13 **Champlain = Samuel de Champlain** (1567–1635): French explorer who founded Quebec City

Michael: Neither did I. *[An idea occurs.]* That's it, maybe that's why we were brought here! *[*Keesic *and* Michael *look at each other.]* To defend Dreamer's Rock.

Keesic: Against what?

Michael: *[Holds up beer bottle.]* This!

Keesic: That!

Rusty *grabs the bottle and puts it in his pack.*

Rusty: It's an empty beer bottle. What's there to defend?

Michael: This particular period of time was known in Aboriginal history as the "Alcoholic Era". From the mid 1800s till the late 1900s, Native people suffered due to an addiction to this liquid. Of course, the problem didn't start and stop at those times. It slowly led up to it then tapered off, much the same way the Black Plague did in medieval Europe.

Keesic: Worse than swamp water.

Rusty: Alcoholic Era? Black Plague? I'm just having a beer, not starting an epidemic.

Michael: When's the last time you consumed enough of this liquid to reach your desired effect?

Rusty: You mean get drunk? Last weekend I guess.

Michael: I thought so.

Rusty: Don't give me that holier-than-thou attitude. You mean to tell me that there is no such thing as beer in the future?

11 **addiction:** state of taking sth. (e.g. drugs or alcohol) as a habit 13 **taper off:** die out slowly

MICHAEL: Of course there is, but people don't die from it any more. Two hundred years of suicide is enough.

RUSTY *shakes his head as he tries to figure* MICHAEL *out.*

RUSTY: How old are you?

MICHAEL: Sixteen. Why?

RUSTY: You sure don't act or talk like you're 16.

MICHAEL: Oh, trust me, I am 16, but I study history. You know what they say, "Those who don't remember the past are condemned to relive it."

KEESIC: But what if it is a good past?

MICHAEL: What?

KEESIC: What if the past you are remembering is a good one? Shouldn't you relive it?

MICHAEL *is stumped.*

MICHAEL: Um …

RUSTY: Ah, this is crazy. *[To* KEESIC.*]* I thought you were bad, he's worse.

KEESIC: Rusty, why is this smelly water you drink so important to you?

RUSTY: *[Really losing his temper.]* It's a beer, not some stupid philosophy, there's nothing to understand. Why is it so hard for you to believe that?

KEESIC: Rusty, why are you so angry all the time?

MICHAEL: All this frustration and aggression. Why?

14 **stumped:** puzzled

RUSTY *almost explodes with frustration.*

RUSTY: Ah, damn, damn, damn, damn, damn.

KEESIC: Nice. Could almost be a chant.

MICHAEL: To some people I think it is.

KEESIC *kneels down beside* RUSTY.

KEESIC: One time when I was young, I don't think I'd seen a dozen winters yet …

MICHAEL: Traditional Native Storytelling! *[He sits, cross-legged, in happy anticipation.]* Please, proceed.

KEESIC *eyes him narrowly before continuing.*

KEESIC: I was gathering bird eggs for my mother. I came across this duck that was splashing around in the water like it had a broken wing. I love duck, so I went after it, but every time I got close it would splash farther away. I followed that duck halfway across the lake before it miraculously healed and flew away. I told my father about this, and he laughed.

RUSTY: And the point is?

MICHAEL *has his arm up, begging to answer the question. He can't restrain himself.*

MICHAEL: Don't you see?! The duck was protecting its eggs, something very delicate and precious to it. It lured Keesic away, a long futile chase to divert his attention. People do the same thing sometimes without knowing it.

RUSTY: I'm trying to save my eggs?

9 **anticipation:** expectation of sth. to come 21 **lure sb. away:** tempt sb. to go somewhere else · **futile:** useless 22 **divert sb.'s attention:** turn sb.'s attention away

MICHAEL: There is something in you that you are protecting with this anger. You are just using it to divert people's attention.

RUSTY: Quack quack.

MICHAEL: What are you afraid of?

RUSTY: I'm not afraid of anything, you idiot.

MICHAEL: *[Confused and disappointed.]* Touchy. I always read that adolescence in this time was supposed to be a time of fun. Drive-in movies, hula hoop, Bay City Rollers. *[Singing.]* S-A-T-U-R-D-A-Y NIGHT!

RUSTY: Bay City Rollers!? Give me a break. You don't know my life, so don't start giving me suggestions on how to run it. Until you've lived my life and felt what I feel, stay off my back.

KEESIC: I don't think you like your life.

RUSTY: Hey, it's the only one I got.

MICHAEL: But is it the one you want?

RUSTY: Do I got a choice? Does it really matter? Okay, I can't go to Hawaii. I'll never own a Porsche, I'll never have all those things I see on television. I'm lucky if I get a new pair of jeans for the first day of school. What's there to be happy for? I'm terrible in school, so I can't walk that side of the tracks, and as for going the traditional Indian route, that's even worse. I hate cleaning fish and I'm a terrible hunter. I don't fit in here. Last year my father took me hunting, I shot my own dog. I can't do anything right except drink. You wanted to know my problems, there they are. I hope you enjoy them.

Everybody is silent for a moment, letting the emotion sink in.

7 **adolescence:** teenager years 8 **Bay City Rollers:** Scottish pop group famous during the 1970s 12 **stay off sb.'s back** (sl.): leave sb. alone

MICHAEL: So that's how you deal with your problems. I must say that I'm not particularly impressed. But here. Have another beer! Everybody has problems, but they cope with them.

RUSTY: Oh yeah? Look at you. I have no idea what kind of outfit that is but it doesn't look like you're too bad off. And judging by the way you talk and the things you've said, you're doing great in school and you know a lot of things. Keesic here only has to worry about hunting enough to eat. They didn't have complicated problems back then. At least you both have your own worlds to fit in and return to. I'm stuck smack-dab in the middle of a family war, between one uncle that's called "Closer" because they say he's closed every bar in Ontario, and my other Uncle Stan, who is basically a powwow Indian, I never know what's going on. Sometimes I don't know if I should go into a sweatlodge or a liquor store. Sometimes they tear me apart. I don't fit in. Like tonight. It's Saturday and what am I doing? Standing on a rock, out in the middle of the woods, talking to two people who probably don't exist. How's that for a social life? Instead of looking at the two of you, I should be out with some hot babe. *[To himself.]* I should have asked her out. I should have.

MICHAEL: Asked who out?

RUSTY: There's a girl I kinda like in town. For all the good it does me.

MICHAEL: What do you mean?

RUSTY: The girl doesn't know I exist. I don't know if it's because I'm Indian or because she thinks I'm a flake. I'm not sure which is worse.

KEESIC: *[Looking puzzled.]* What's an Indian?

Both RUSTY *and* MICHAEL *look at* KEESIC.

RUSTY: Oh, that's right, you've never heard the word.

10 **smack-dab in the middle of sth.:** right in the middle of sth. 12 **powwow** ['paʊwaʊ]: festival of North American Indians • **powwow Indian:** (here) sb. who follows the powwow summer circuit 14 **sweatlodge:** structure where one purifies oneself through sweat and prayer 24 **flake** (NAmE sl.): uninteresting person

MICHAEL: It's a generic term used to describe all original inhabitants of this land. It was popular up until approximately 100 years ago, my time. In fact, right around your time. *[Points to* RUSTY.*]* The more politically correct terms in this day and age are "Native" or "Aboriginal".

KEESIC: So we are all … Indian?

RUSTY: Yup.

KEESIC: Why would an Indian girl not like you for being Indian?

RUSTY: She's not.

KEESIC: She's one of these white people?

RUSTY: Uh huh.

KEESIC: Interesting. What does she look like?

RUSTY: Her name is Sherry. Doesn't that sound great? Oh, she's real pretty. She's got long blonde hair …

KEESIC: Blonde?

RUSTY: Yellow.

RUSTY, *feeling more at ease, is exploding with energy. He does a hand spring to shake himself out of it.*

KEESIC: White people got yellow hair? Just like the sun?

RUSTY: *[Smiling.]* And twice as hot.

RUSTY *begins moving along the edge of the rock, balancing himself. It's a sort of game with him, one that* KEESIC *and* MICHAEL *join in.* MICHAEL *has no talent for this, however, and is rather slow.*

1 **generic:** general 17–18 **hand spring:** jump in which a person lands on their hands

KEESIC: During the summer, when my family joins other families to hunt and fish, there's always this girl that would be at the camp. Her name is Nungohns. For the past few summers now, we've watched each other, always from a distance. We talk, but that's about it.

RUSTY: So what's the problem? Just date the girl. You make it sound like it's a terrible thing. What's the matter? Her parents don't like you?

KEESIC: We are of the same clan.

RUSTY: That's like being in the same family, isn't it?

KEESIC: Families are recognized by what clan they belong to. They represent a particular family grouping, and you are not allowed to hunt or eat the flesh of your clan animal. And you cannot marry someone from your clan.

MICHAEL: Are you related to her?

KEESIC: Many generations ago, but we might as well be total strangers for all that it matters.

RUSTY: No way of getting around it?

KEESIC: It is not permitted.

MICHAEL: Maybe you and this Mongoose could elope.

KEESIC and RUSTY: Nungohns!

MICHAEL: Sorry.

KEESIC: If I could turn our backs on our family's ways, where would we go? I don't know about here, but where I come from, two people alone in the bush may survive the summer, but not the winter. Not when you no longer exist in the village's eyes. What if something bad happens, who do you go to for help? That's the way it is.

18 **mongoose:** small animal that kills snakes · **elope** (v.): run away with sb. to get married

All three are lying back on the rock, legs dangling over the edge.

RUSTY: Well, at least your girl likes you. As for mine, I might as well be a doorknob.

MICHAEL: Where do you know this girl from?

RUSTY: School, where else? It's one of the only reasons I go any more.

MICHAEL: Obviously you don't like school.

RUSTY: Nothing gets past you, Sherlock. It's just that I have a problem trying to figure out why I should care when Napoleon became emperor of France.

MICHAEL: 1799, I believe.

KEESIC: Who is Napoleon?

RUSTY: Some French guy.

KEESIC: What's a French guy?

MICHAEL: All knowledge matters. In order for the mind to grow it must consume a variety of subjects. Your mind is just like your body, if you only eat one type of food, you die.

RUSTY: My mother's been living on Kraft Dinner for the past 10 years and she's still kicking.

MICHAEL: Oh, be serious!

KEESIC: Will Rusty ever need this knowledge of Nap … Nap …

RUSTY: Napoleon.

KEESIC: Napoleon.

17 **Kraft Dinner:** ready-made meals 18 **kicking** (sl.): alive

MICHAEL: Granted he may never find a practical use for such knowledge, but it could influence other thoughts he may have.

RUSTY: I like being *[Stressing the joke.]* under the influence. Ah, screw Napoleon, hey, Obi-Michael Kenobi, you got girl or school problems where you come from?

MICHAEL: I have what could be referred to as a girlfriend. So far anyways.

RUSTY: That don't sound good.

MICHAEL: It isn't. She's not impressed with my preoccupation with the past. She'd rather I be more pragmatic and less, less … what's the word … less airy, theoretical, esoteric … I hesitate to use the word "spiritual".

RUSTY: Geez, you use a lot of big words.

MICHAEL: It's important to be accurate.

RUSTY: Sounds like you got money and power. I wish I had your problems. You want to stay here while I go back to your place?

MICHAEL: *[Sadly.]* What do they say in this time, it ain't all peachy keen. We've lost our culture. It really isn't there. It's all been explained away or forgotten or just walked away from. Even our cheekbones are going. The poverty that once plagued us is gone, but at what cost? The language only exists on digital discs, the sweatlodge is gone, and Dreamer's Rock is a tourist attraction.

KEESIC: How can so much be lost?

RUSTY: I don't know.

MICHAEL: I used to come here when I was a kid. I still do. *[He pulls some sweetgrass from his pocket.]* I'm the only one on the reserve

4 **Obi Kenobi:** character in the film *Star Wars* 17 **peachy keen** (NAmE sl.): easy and good 20 **plague sb.:** trouble sb. 26 **sweetgrass:** herb used for specific Indian rituals

who has any sweetgrass, and I think I'm the only one who knows how to find it.

RUSTY: Where did you get it?

MICHAEL: In the field that overlooks the island in the bay. It's the only place left on the reserve.

RUSTY: Hey, I know that place. I used to pick sweetgrass there with my aunt. You can smell it 10 minutes before you get there.

MICHAEL: That hasn't changed.

RUSTY: Smells good.

MICHAEL: There are plans to turn the field into a helipad.

RUSTY: That's bizarre. Well, maybe I can leave you a little time capsule there.

MICHAEL: You did!

RUSTY: I did?

MICHAEL: Two years ago, I found a capsule protruding from the ground. In it I found some material addressed to me, dated 2023. Needless to say I was greatly surprised.

RUSTY: And I left it? In 2023? What did I leave?

MICHAEL: Something very interesting. It was sort of responsible for igniting my interest in the past.

KEESIC *takes the sweetgrass, examines it, and smells it.*

KEESIC: This is the first sweetgrass you've picked?

10 **helipad:** place where a helicopter lands 11 **time capsule:** container buried in the ground containing sth. (e.g. coins, newspaper) to be dug up at a future date 15 **protrude from sth.:** stick out of sth. 20 **ignite sth.:** (here) start sth.

MICHAEL: No, but it always ends up the same, falling apart into a mess.

KEESIC: You don't braid it?

MICHAEL: I have a problem with tactile maneuvering.

KEESIC *starts to braid the sweetgrass.* RUSTY *intrudes rudely.*

RUSTY: To heck with your tactical maneuvers and your sweetgrass. Cough it up, buddy. What did I leave in that there time capsule?

MICHAEL: Just some material, that's all.

RUSTY: No, no, no, no, no. You said "something very interesting". What is "something very interesting", Michael?

MICHAEL: I don't think I should tell you.

RUSTY: Well, I do. If I left it, it's my property.

MICHAEL: In 2023?

RUSTY: That's beside the point.

MICHAEL: No, that is the point. Then I think you were ready to leave it, ready to share it.

RUSTY: *[Frustrated.]* "It". What is "it"?

MICHAEL: You're getting angry again.

KEESIC *looks up from his sweetgrass braiding.*

KEESIC: See how you are?

RUSTY *growls.*

2 **braid sth.:** etwas flechten 3 **tactile maneuvering:** (here) using one's hands 5 **heck** (sl.): hell 6 **cough sth. up** (sl.): talk about sth.

MICHAEL: If I tell you the future, your future, it may change things.

RUSTY: Too late. I know about you, don't I? What's the difference with this?

MICHAEL: This information will affect your life, maybe negatively in this crucial and formative stage. I don't think it's advisable at the moment.

RUSTY *nearly strangles* MICHAEL.

RUSTY: You think you're hot stuff, huh? Give a guy a little information and he starts wanting to play government, telling you only what he thinks you need to know. If you're so smart, go check out that hollow in 2095. I'll leave you another time capsule there.

KEESIC *looks over the cliff.*

KEESIC: That's poison ivy.

RUSTY: Yeah, and I'll bet he's just itching to find out the significance of that, huh?

MICHAEL: I don't believe you're the same Rusty.

RUSTY: As what, Buck Rogers?

MICHAEL: The wit is still there, but not the control. Until you find some control, I don't think you're ready for the future.

RUSTY: Fine. You keep your future. I'll find out mine soon enough, in 30 years.

MICHAEL: Thirty-four.

RUSTY: Whatever.

MICHAEL: It's best to be precise.

5 **crucial:** important · **formative:** relating to one's growth and development 9 **hollow** (n.): hole 12 **poison ivy:** plant which causes a rash (= Ausschlag) 16 **Buck Rogers:** science fiction cartoon character hero of the 1930s

RUSTY: Look, I don't need your information and I don't want it.

MICHAEL *approaches him, about to say something.*

RUSTY: Stop! Don't even mention the subject to me again. Even if you begged me to let you tell me everything you know, I wouldn't even listen. Jerk!

RUSTY *jumps to another, isolated place on the rock and pouts. By this time,* KEESIC *has braided the sweetgrass and now offers it to* MICHAEL.

MICHAEL: *[Touched.]* Thank you.

KEESIC: Have you ever used it to smudge?

MICHAEL: I know it's to purify yourself, but other than that, I don't know how.

KEESIC: No language. No dream quests. No rituals. Isn't there anything left? Warriors!

RUSTY: Sorry, but there are no more warriors.

KEESIC: No warriors? No battles? What about the Nodwheg? Surely you must fight them.

MICHAEL: The what?

RUSTY: Iroquois. Mohawk, to be exact. No, we're friends with them now.

KEESIC: *[Horrified.]* With the Nodwheg? No!

RUSTY: Sorry to tell you this, buddy, but I was at a baseball tournament of theirs just a few weeks ago.

KEESIC: If there are no more warriors, how does a young man get honor?

5 **jerk** (sl.): idiot 6 **pout:** schmollen 9 **smudge** (v.): Indian ritual of making oneself pure through smoke

RUSTY: Honor means different things to different people. My uncle says the most honorable thing he ever did was marry my aunt.

KEESIC: But what about bravery?

RUSTY: You ever met my aunt?

KEESIC: So much is different. Do we still eat food?

RUSTY: Are you kidding? I don't have an uncle under 250 pounds or an aunt under 200. Does that answer your question?

KEESIC: Good. It's nice to know that hasn't changed.

KEESIC *rubs his stomach. Mentioning food has made him remember his hunger.*

MICHAEL: Are you hungry?

KEESIC: I haven't eaten much in the last three days. Winters can be hard, and so can hunger. I wish I had some muskrat. That's my favorite food.

MICHAEL: I could never understand the fascination of eating the flesh of animals that come from a swamp. I find it disgusting.

RUSTY: Be nice. I'm kinda partial to moose. Especially moose burgers.

KEESIC: My father would always let me have the first slice from a kill. I would always pray to the Great Spirit that his hunt would be successful. Then there's pheasant.

RUSTY: Mmmmmmmm.

KEESIC: Although many times we go hungry. Sometimes we drink only teas for days. The winters can be long.

13 **muskrat:** Bisamratte 17 **be partial to sth.** [pɑːʃl]: enjoy sth. · **moose:** Elch
20 **pheasant:** Fasan

RUSTY: Boy, I thought I had it hard. I've never really been hungry. The hardest thing I ever had to deal with was my father.

KEESIC: Your father?

RUSTY: Yeah, he has a great backhand, and I don't mean tennis. One of the scariest times of my life was just after I turned 12. I found out I couldn't fit under the bed and had to find a new place to hide. Well, at least I can outrun him now.

KEESIC: Your father hurt you? I don't understand. Why?

RUSTY: I don't know. Go ask him.

KEESIC: But children are a gift from the Creator. They are put here for a purpose.

RUSTY: Yeah, well, he had a purpose for me all right.

KEESIC *slaps* MICHAEL *to get his attention.*

KEESIC: And you?

MICHAEL: Not in my family, but yeah, it still exists in some places.

KEESIC: The more I hear the more is lost.

MICHAEL: Oh, come on. It's not all that bad. Believe me. Look at me!

KEESIC *and* RUSTY *laugh helplessly.* MICHAEL'*s feelings are a little hurt.*

MICHAEL: I lead a happy life. I'm graduating top of my class. No problems.

RUSTY: I thought you said everybody's got problems?

MICHAEL: I did, didn't I?

7 outrun sb.: run faster than sb.

KEESIC: So nothing is wrong in your world? Everything is fine? People don't hurt? Everybody is happy?

MICHAEL: We're only allowed to swim one week a summer.

KEESIC: One week a summer?

RUSTY: You're kidding. Why?

MICHAEL: That's when they purify the lake. It only lasts a week and then the water goes bad again. There's a new type of algae that thrives on ultraviolet rays and pollution. The lake is covered all summer long like a green blanket. But for the past three years there's been a festival on the island called Swimming Days. I envy the two of you. Being able to swim anywhere. Even drink the water. It must be wonderful.

RUSTY: Gee, I never thought about it before.

KEESIC: And you call this no problem?

MICHAEL: It's called keeping things in perspective.

KEESIC: Perspective. Perspective. I don't like this word, perspective.

MICHAEL *is enjoying the sun.*

MICHAEL: This sun makes me feel very much alive. You know, in many ways, we're all very much alike.

RUSTY: I hate to disappoint you there, Michael, but look at the three of us. We ain't nothing alike. What we got in common you could stuff in my underwear.

KEESIC: That small, huh?

MICHAEL: We're all Indian.

KEESIC: I am Odawa, not this "Indian".

7 thrive on sth.: grow by living off sth.

MICHAEL: Okay then, we're all Odawa.

KEESIC: No.

MICHAEL: Pardon?

KEESIC: No. I don't think you are Odawa. Or you, either. Everything I have heard today is not Odawa.

RUSTY: Hey, I was born on the reserve. I am so Odawa and Ojibway. I got a card and everything.

KEESIC: It's more than blood. I am very saddened by what has happened to my people.

MICHAEL: We've survived and we're getting stronger.

KEESIC: Then why are we speaking this English? Do we not have our old tongue? The Odawa tongue? Why are we speaking this English? Is this the language of these white people?

MICHAEL: That's not fair. I wanted to learn the language, but nobody speaks it anymore.

KEESIC: *[To Rusty.]* Do you speak your language?

RUSTY: I can count up to 10. Next year though, I'm taking the language in school. There's a new course.

KEESIC: A course? In school? What does that mean?

RUSTY: I guess it means I'll be spending an hour a day in school learning to speak Indian.

KEESIC: You take time out to learn it? Why is it not spoken freely in your villages?

RUSTY: I don't know. I guess there's not a need for it any more. English is spoken everywhere and we were sort of dragged along with it.

KEESIC: But our language is formed by our thoughts. Our thinking forms our words. I do not like this language, English. There is no beauty in it. In our language, when you talk about the earth or the forest, you can smell the leaves around you, feel the grass beneath your feet. Until our language is spoken again and rituals and ceremonies followed, then there are no more Odawa.

MICHAEL: That's not fair. I know I'm Indian. Just because I don't like muskrat or moose meat is no reason to say I'm not Indian.

KEESIC: Odawa.

MICHAEL: Odawa then.

MICHAEL *pushes* KEESIC*'s shoulder in frustration. Retaliating,* KEESIC *pushes* MICHAEL *and a fight ensues.* RUSTY *gets in there and is attacked by both boys. He extricates himself quickly.*

RUSTY: Okay, okay, fine.

MICHAEL: Every culture must progress. You'd be amazed and pleased to see what we've achieved. Odawa are no longer starving in the bush, or dying of some disease. We are in control of our own destiny.

KEESIC: But weren't we always?

MICHAEL: Not until we achieved self-government in the 2020s.

KEESIC: Self-government? When did we lose it?

MICHAEL: In the late 1700s and early 1800s I believe.

KEESIC: What happened to us?

2 **drag along with sth.:** not have enough strength to fight sth. 13 **retaliate:** fight back 14 **ensue:** result 15 **extricate oneself:** free oneself from sth. 18 **starve:** die of hunger

MICHAEL: We sold our land, signed treaties with the white government and were put on reserves of land and left there to die.

KEESIC: But not any more?

MICHAEL: No. We control our own paths again.

KEESIC: At what cost? We lost ourselves to regain something we shouldn't have lost in the first place. There are no more Odawa.

MICHAEL: How can you say that? It's not true.

KEESIC: An Odawa would never let anybody take the land.

MICHAEL: They did.

KEESIC: They did not.

RUSTY: They did, Keesic.

KEESIC: They did not. I don't believe you. What would they have to gain by selling the land? Something nobody can own?

MICHAEL: Some of these white people got them drunk and made them sign something called treaties.

KEESIC: Drunk? With this thing called beer?

MICHAEL: Something like that. Others signed to save their people, to keep what little land they could to live on.

KEESIC: Didn't they fight?

MICHAEL: They did, but there were too many of them.

KEESIC: I can't believe they are more powerful than the Odawa.

6 in the first place: (here) anyway

MICHAEL: In some ways they were. But you're wrong, Keesic. No matter what you may think of us, we still exist. Changed, but Odawa.

KEESIC: You may have Odawa blood in your veins but do you have the heart to pump it?

MICHAEL: We're better Odawa than you ever were.

KEESIC: I don't think so.

MICHAEL: It was an Odawa doctor who discovered the cure for the common cold.

KEESIC: We never had the common cold.

RUSTY: For two people who claim to know so much about us, you sure are stupid.

MICHAEL: If anybody here were to be classified as stupid, I'm sure it would be you.

RUSTY *looks at* MICHAEL, *then at* KEESIC, *then at the vista of his home.*

RUSTY: Where are we standing?

MICHAEL: Pardon?

RUSTY: Where are we standing?

KEESIC *and* MICHAEL *look at each other, confused.*

We're on Dreamer's Rock. And what is Dreamer's Rock a part of? *[More confused looks.]* It's part of the land, part of Mother Earth. My Uncle Stan once told me that it all comes back to that. The Odawa, and I guess other Indians, are the land, of the land. The land is the basis for everything. We have survived not just on the land, but with it.

KEESIC: How can you know the meaning of survival, you who have never known hunger?

RUSTY: I survive in my time, you survive in yours. You do it by hunting in the bush, I do it by working in a snack bar, and he probably does it through space-age stuff. The tools may change but the idea stays the same. The point is, we've survived. We're still here today.

MICHAEL: And tomorrow.

RUSTY *pauses as he collects his thoughts.*

RUSTY: Yesterday I wouldn't have thought all this was possible. Yesterday it would have been another day of the Flintstones, working at the snack bar, and maybe a beer afterwards.

MICHAEL: And now?

RUSTY: All I know is I came up here to get drunk and be alone for a while. So much for that idea. I never thought about all this Indian stuff before. I just sort of took it for granted. I guess I have some more thinking to do. I think the main thing about being Indian or Odawa is … we're better-looking.

All the boys smile.

KEESIC: That will always be true.

RUSTY: Some things will never change.

MICHAEL: Rusty.

RUSTY: Yo Dude, what can I do for you?

MICHAEL: I have something I want to give you. Actually, I'm returning it to you, even before you gave it to me.

10 **the Flintstones:** die Familie Feuerstein 15 **take sth. for granted:** be so familiar with sth. that one no longer appreciates it 22 **yo dude** (sl.): yes mate

MICHAEL *gives him a small, rusted container.*

RUSTY: What is it?

He opens it, takes out an old newspaper clipping and reads.

RUSTY: This says I'm going to be the first Grand Chief of the Aboriginal Government. And it's dated 2023. I'll be 50 years old. *[It sinks in.]* Holy. I'll be old. Damn. Guess this means I have to go back to school. And I thought I'd be free next year.

KEESIC: All things come with a price, Rusty.

RUSTY: *[Awed.]* Wow. Me, Grand Chief.

KEESIC: That's a pretty powerful title, Rusty. I hope you can find it in yourself to live up to it.

RUSTY: I can't even drive a car yet and already I'm running a government.

KEESIC *takes something from around his neck. It is a hide pouch.*

KEESIC: I, too, am not without a gift. I want you to wear it around your neck.

RUSTY: What is it?

KEESIC: Weekah root. It will keep you strong and healthy.

KEESIC *places it around* RUSTY*'s neck.* RUSTY *fingers the pouch.*

RUSTY: Thanks, guys. Thanks a lot, but I don't have anything to give you.

MICHAEL: Don't worry, your time to give will come.

The sound of the crow cawing can be heard again.

3 **clipping:** article cut out of a newspaper 14 **hide pouch:** small bag made from leather, usually worn around the neck 18 **Weekah root:** type of herb

KEESIC: Rusty, this is your summer. And spring belongs before it, and fall afterwards. Every season has its time and I think it's time to return to those places. I think Toronto has come to an end.

RUSTY *holds his hand out in an effort to shake* KEESIC'*s hand.*

RUSTY: It's been interesting, Keesic. That's all I can say.

KEESIC *looks puzzled at* RUSTY'*s outstretched hand.*

MICHAEL: You're supposed to shake hands.

KEESIC *looks at his own hand and shakes it vigorously like he's trying to get something off it.* RUSTY *and* MICHAEL *laugh as* RUSTY *grabs* KEESIC'*s hand. Suddenly, when they touch, they are all thrown to the ground.* KEESIC *starts to cough again.* RUSTY *slaps him on the back.*

RUSTY: You okay? Hey man, you all right?

KEESIC: Stat-ta-ha. Ngashtoon chi nishnaabemyaan miinwaa. [I can speak my language again.]

RUSTY: I thought you said you couldn't speak it any more.

KEESIC *speaks to them in Indian, telling them they must pray. He places the boys carefully, facing the east, and begins a final prayer of thanksgiving to the Creator for allowing them to meet across time on this sacred spot.*

At the end of the prayer, RUSTY *sinks to the rock, holds his weekah pouch with one hand and drums a beat on the rock with the other. He sings a song in Indian about hearing the voice of the people, so far away. During the song,* MICHAEL *and* KEESIC *leave the rock and disappear within it. At the end of the song,* RUSTY *opens his eyes. He is alone. He goes to pick up his knapsack and beneath it he finds a crow feather. He holds the feather up to the sky, turning four times, saluting the Four Directions. Then he moves off. Just before leaving, he places his hand respectfully on the rock.*

Ah, meeg-wetch. [Thank you.]

Additional Texts

Pretty Like a White Boy: The Adventures of a Blue-Eyed Ojibway

In this big, huge world, with all its billions and billions of people, it's safe to say that everybody will eventually come across personalities and individuals that will touch them in some peculiar yet poignant way. Individuals that in some way represent and help define who you are. I'm no different, mine was Kermit the Frog. Not just because Natives have a long tradition of savouring Frogs' legs, but because of his music. If you all may remember, Kermit is quite famous for his rendition of "It's Not Easy Being Green". I can relate. If I could sing, my song would be "It's Not Easy Having Blue Eyes in a Brown-Eyed Village".

Yes, I'm afraid it's true. The author happens to be a card-carrying Indian. Once you get past the aforementioned eyes, the fair skin, light brown hair, and noticeable lack of cheekbones, there lies the heart and spirit of an Ojibway storyteller. Honest Injun, or as the more politically correct term may be, honest aboriginal.

You see, I'm the product of a white father I never knew, and an Ojibway woman who evidently couldn't run fast enough. As a kid I knew I looked a bit different. But, then again, all kids are paranoid when it comes to their peers. I had a fairly happy childhood, frolicking through the bullrushes. But there were certain things that, even then, made me notice my unusual appearance. Whenever we played cowboys and Indians, guess who had to be the bad guy, the cowboy.

It wasn't until I left the Reserve for the big bad city, that I became more aware of the role people expected me to play, and the fact that physically I didn't fit in. Everybody seemed to have this preconceived idea of how every Indian looked and acted. One guy, on my first day of college, asked me what kind of horse I preferred. I didn't have the heart to tell him "hobby".

I've often tried to be philosophical about the whole thing. I have both white and red blood in me, I guess that makes me pink. I am a "Pink"

5 **peculiar:** strange · **poignant:** affecting one's feelings deeply 8 **savour:** eat with enjoyment 9 **rendition:** presentation, performance 20 **peer:** person of the same age and background · **frolick:** play happily 21 **bullrush:** kind of tall reed or rush 26 **preconceived:** (of an idea) formed in advance 29 **hobby horse:** Steckenpferd

man. Try to imagine this, I'm walking around on any typical Reserve in Canada, my head held high, proudly announcing to everyone "I am a Pink Man". It's a good thing I ran track in school.

My pinkness is constantly being pointed out to me over and over and over again. "You don't look Indian?" "You're not Indian, are you?" "Really?!?" I got questions like that from both white and Native people, for a while I debated having my status card tattooed on my forehead.

And like most insecure people and specially a blue-eyed Native writer, I went through a particularly severe identity crisis at one point. In fact, I admit it, one depressing spring evening, I died my hair black. Pitch black.

The reason for such a dramatic act, you may ask? Show Business. You see, for the last eight years or so, I've worked in various capacities in the performing arts, and as a result I'd always get calls to be an extra or even try out for an important role in some Native oriented movie. This anonymous voice would phone, having been given my number, and ask if I would be interested in trying out for a movie. Being a naturally ambitious, curious, and greedy young man, I would always readily agree, stardom flashing im my eyes and hunger pains from my wallet.

A few days later I would show up for the audition, and that was always an experience. What kind of experience you may ask? Picture this, the picture calls for the casting of seventeenth-century Mohawk warriors living in a traditional longhouse. The casting director calls the name "Drew Hayden Taylor" and I enter.

The casting director, the producer, and the film's director look up from the table and see my face, blue eyes flashing in anticipation. I once was described as a slightly chubby beachboy. But even beachboys have tans. Anyway, there would be a quick flush of confusion, a recheck of the papers, and a hesitant "Mr Taylor?" Then they would ask if I was at the right audition. It was always the same. By the way, I never got any of the parts I tried for, except for a few anonymous crowd shots. Politics tells me it's because of the way I look, reality tells me it's probably because I can't act. I'm not sure which is better.

It's not just film people either. Recently I've become quite involved in Theatre, Native theatre to be exact. And one cold October day I was happily attending the Toronto leg of a province-wide tour of my first play, *Toronto at Dreamer's Rock*. The place was sold out, the audience

7 **debate sth.:** consider sth. 11 **pitch black:** pechschwarz 27 **chubby:** plump, fat
31 **crowd shot:** Massenszene

very receptive and the performance was wonderful. Ironically one of the actors was also half white.

The director later told me he had been talking with the actor's father, an older non-Native type chap. Evidently he had asked a few questions about me, and how I did my research. This made the director curious and he asked about his interest. He replied, "He's got an amazing grasp of the Native situation for a white person."

Not all these incidents are work related either. One time a friend and I were coming out of a rather upscale bar (we were out Yuppie watching) and managed to catch a cab. We thanked the cab driver for being so comfortably close on such a cold night, he shrugged and nonchalantly talked about knowing what bars to drive around. "If you're not careful, all you'll get is drunk Indians." I hiccuped.

Another time this cab driver droned on and on about the government. He started out by criticizing Mulroney, and eventually to his handling of the Oka crisis. This perked up my ears, until he said "If it were me, I'd have tear-gassed the place by the second day. No more problem." He got a dime tip. A few incidents like this and I'm convinced I'd make a great undercover agent for one of the Native political organizations.

But then again, even Native people have been known to look at me with a fair amount of suspicion. Many years ago when I was a young man, I was working on a documentary on Native culture up in the wilds of Northern Ontario. We were at an isolated cabin filming a trapper woman and her kids. This one particular nine-year-old girl seemed to take a shine to me. She followed me around for two days both annoying me and endearing herself to me. But she absolutely refused to believe that I was Indian. The whole film crew tried to tell her but to no avail. She was certain I was white.

Then one day as I was loading up the car with film equipment, she asked me if I wanted some tea. Being in a hurry I declined the tea. She

1 **receptive:** willing to accept sth. 6 **grasp** (n.): understanding, insight 9 **upscale:** trendy, chic 11 **nonchalent:** calm and casual 14 **drone on** (infml.): talk continually in a boring tone 15 **Brian Mulroney** (born 1939): Conservative prime minister of Canada (1984–1988) 16 **Oka crisis:** in 1990 there was an armed conflict between Mohawks and the Quebec government over the extension of a golf club on land held sacred by the Mohawks · **perk up one's ears** (idm.): listen 18 **dime:** coin worth 10 cents 24 **cabin:** small hut made of wood · **trapper:** person who catches animals to sell the fur 26 **take a shine to sb.** (infml.): like sb. 28 **to no avail:** without success 31 **decline sth.:** refuse to accept sth.

immediately smiled with victory crying out "See, you're not Indian, all Indians drink tea!"

Frustrated and a little hurt I whipped out my Status card and thrust it at her. Now there I was, standing in a Northern Ontario winter, showing my Status card to a nine-year-old non-status Indian girl who had no idea what one was. Looking back, this may not have been one of my brighter moves.

But I must admit, it was a Native woman that boiled everything down in one simple sentence. You may know that woman, Marianne Jones from *The Beachcombers* television series. We were working on a film together out west and we got to gossiping. Eventually we got around to talking about our respective villages. Hers on the Queen Charlotte Islands, or Haida Gwaii as the Haida call them, and mine in central Ontario.

Eventually childhood on the Reserve was being discussed and I made a comment about the way I look. She studied me for a moment, smiled, and said, "Do you know what the old women in my village would call you?" Hesitant but curious, I shook my head. "They'd say you were pretty like a white boy." To this day I'm still not sure if I like that.

Now some may argue that I am simply a Métis with a Status card. I disagree, I failed French in grade 11. And the Métis as everyone knows have their own separate and honourable culture, particularly in western Canada. And of course I am well aware that I am not the only person with my physical characteristics.

I remember once looking at a video tape of a drum group, shot on a Reserve up near Manitoulin Island. I noticed one of the drummers seemed quite fairhaired, almost blond. I mentioned this to my girlfriend of the time and she shrugged saying, "Well, that's to be expected. The highway runs right through the Reserve."

Perhaps I'm being too critical. There's a lot to be said for both cultures. For example, on the left hand, you have the Native respect for elders. They understand the concept of wisdom and insight coming with age.

On the white hand, there's Italian food. I mean I really love my mother and family but seriously, does anything really beat good Veal Scallopini? Most of my aboriginal friends share my fondness for this

3 **whip sth. out** (infml.): take sth. out quickly **11 gossip** (v.): chat about other people **20 Métis:** person with mixed blood (esp. French and Native American) **35 veal:** meat of a calf

particular brand of food. Wasn't there a warrior at Oka named Lasagna? I found it ironic, though curiously logical, that Columbus was Italian. A connection I wonder?

Also Native people have this wonderful respect and love for the land. They believe they are part of it, a mere chain in the cycle of existence. Now as many of you know, this conflicts with the accepted Judeo-Christian, i.e. western view, of land management. I even believe somewhere in the first chapters of the Bible it says something about God giving man dominion over Nature. Check it out, Genesis 4:?, "Thou shalt clear cut." So I grew up understanding that everything around me is important and alive. My Native heritage gave me that.

And again, on the white hand, there's breast implants. Darn clever them white people. That's something Indians would never have invented, seriously. We're not ambitious enough. We just take what the Creator decides to give us, but no, not the white man. Just imagine it, some serious looking white man, and let's face it, people, we know it was a man who invented them, don't we? So just imagine some serious looking white doctor sitting around in his laboratory muttering to himself, "Big tits, big tits, hmm, how do I make big tits?" If it was an Indian, it would be "Big tits, big tits, white women sure got big tits" and leave it at that.

So where does that leave me on the big philosophical scoreboard, what exactly are my choices again; Indians – respect for elders, love of the land. White people – food and big tits. In order to live in both cultures I guess I'd have to find an Indian woman with big tits who lives with her grandmother in a cabin out in the woods and can make Fettuccini Alfredo on a wood stove.

Now let me make this clear, I'm not writing this for sympathy, or out of anger, or even some need for self-glorification. I am just setting the facts straight. For as you read this, a new Nation is born. This is a declaration of independence, my declaration of independence.

I've spent too many years explaining who and what I am repeatedly, so as of this moment, I officially secede from both races. I plan to start my own separate nation. Because I am half Ojibway, and half Caucasian, we will be called the Occasions. And I of course, since I'm founding the new nation, will be a Special Occasion.

(First appeared in This Magazine, *August 1991.)*

9 **dominion:** power 10 **clear cut:** kahlschlagen 22 **scoreboard:** board which shows the scores while a match is being played 33 **secede from sth.:** break away from sth.

Climbing onto the Band Wagon

Some time during that ancient age known collectively as the sixties, there lived in the United States a black activist and writer by the name of Eldridge Cleaver. And this man noticed an unusual trend developing in the mating rituals of those tempestuous times. It became apparent to him that more and more white women, specifically blondish types, seemed to be dating an awful lot of black men, and vice versa.

He chalked it up to these women wanting to rebel against the restrictive social norms of middle-class life, to upset their parents and the status quo of the day; such rebelliousness seemed to be in vogue. He also reasoned that the black men, wanting to sample the privileged world that had been denied them by the dominant white society, thought this was great. Who were they to argue?

And because this cross-cultural dating trend was first discussed in Mr. Cleaver's book *Soul On Ice,* it has been referred to, in some circles, as the Soul-On-Ice Syndrome. I think the name says it all.

That was in the sixties. This is the nineties, and the more things change, the more they stay the same. Except this time, the trendy thing happens to involve Native people: Finding an aboriginal companion seems to be all the rage. So, in the name of social commentary, I would like to name this courting phenomenon the Spirit-On-Ice Syndrome.

But we're not just talking about dating, we're talking about the whole enchilada (if I may appropriate that cultural metaphor). It seems that ever since *Dances with Wolves* and *Dry Lips Oughto Move to Kapuskasing* hit the public, the white world has been beating a path to the reserve door, seeking spiritual fulfilment, elders' wisdom and discount cigarettes.

Recently an elder from my community told me about a visit by two white women to his house. These were the most recent in a regular influx of what he calls "wannabes, groupies and do-gooders" who said (I paraphrase their words), "I-really-respect-and-honour-your-culture-and -want-to-be-a-part-of-it-so-please-let-me-participate-and-learn-from-your-sacred-and-ancient-ceremonies -so-I-can-understand-your-ways-this-isn't-just -a-phase-I'm-going-through-I-really-mean-it-so-can-I-huh?"

1 **climb onto a band wagon:** join sth. which is very popular 5 **mating ritual:** Paarungsritual · **tempestuous:** stormy 8 **chalk sth. up to sth. else:** consider that sth. is caused by sth. else 21 **court** (v.): look for a partner 23 **enchilada:** type of Mexican food; (here) subject 30 **wannabe** (sl.) = **want-to-be:** person who wants to be like sb. else

My elder friend and I sat around for a good 45 minutes trying to figure out what, specifically, they wanted to "understand". Why we eat so much macaroni and tomatoes? Why 75 per cent of the Native population doesn't vote? Why we wear buckskin on hot summer days? (I haven't figured that one out yet myself.)

This one blond woman who was visiting my friend had recently been divorced from a black gentleman. (I wonder if they met during the sixties.) Now she was becoming fascinated with Native culture and, I guess, Native men. At one point, she said, her parents had asked her if she was ever going to date a white man, to which she replied, "I doubt it. They have no mystery."

Mystery? That was good for another 45-minute conversation with my elder friend.

What mystery? We get up in the morning, put our clothes on, have coffee (usually fully or extra-caffeinated), go to the bathroom ... Yes, Indians do go to the bathroom, but in a secret Indian way that can't be revealed. Maybe that's what she was talking about.

There are many more of these people than you might expect. A friend of mine went out west last summer to attend a sun dance. When she arrived, she was one of the few Natives there; 80 per cent of the people setting up camp were non-Native. She was somewhat peeved.

There's also the story of this woman who went to Mexico, became enamoured of a Mexican Native Indian who sneaked her onto the grounds of one of the Aztec ruins. There he told her about an ancient Aztec ceremony that involved making love on the steps of the pyramid. She believed and they did.

Stories like this remind me that I'm only half an hour from the Peterborough petroglyphs. Hmmmm ...

And there was the time I met this woman, quite casually, who was opening a Native art gallery. She introduced herself as being from the Six Nations Reserve in Southern Ontario. Several weeks later I asked her which of the six nations she was – Mohawk, Cayuga, etc. She looked at me for a moment, then confessed that she was actually married into the reserve (now divorced) but that she was quite proud of the fact she still had her status card.

A few weeks later she started dating an Alaskan Native painter, went to visit him, received an Indian name and refused to be called by her

21 **peeved:** annoyed 22–23 **become enamoured of sb.:** fall in love with sb. 23 **sneak sb. to sth.:** lead sb. secretly to sth. 28 **Peterborough:** town in the province of Ontario · **petroglyph:** drawing or carving on a rock

English name. She had her brand, spanking new Indian name put on her business cards.

Is it any wonder my elder friend and I are a little cynical? After 501 years of oppression, destruction and general annoyance, we are now, overnight, chic. Irony can be painful.

But I should be fair. Not all white people who come into our communities can be classified this way. I have one aunt (who's French) who speaks better Ojibway than I do and has a thicker accent than me. And she didn't show up on our reserve all those years ago to "understand" – she just fell in love and couldn't have cared less whether my uncle was Indian. I have many other relatives and friends who fit this category. They accept us as who we are, but they don't want to be us. Who can argue with that?

We also mustn't forget that there are some Native people out there who for one reason or another want to be white. So we're willing to make you a deal. Ship ours back, and we'll ship yours back too.

(First appeared in The Globe and Mail, *August 6, 1993.)*

An Indian by Any Other Name

The other day, I, a reasonably well-educated man of the ever-more-complex nineties, made a tremendous political and social *faux pas*: I referred to myself and other people of my ethnic background as "Indians".

Oh, the shame of it. You could hear the gasp echo across the room.

It was done, I assure you, with the most innocent intention, but nevertheless, I was soon castigated by both my brethren and, in my humble opinion, the overly politically sensitive members of other cultural groups. And the white people.

Needless to say, in these politically correct times, I was inundated by these same people with criticism about the use of such an outdated term. "We're/You're no longer called Indians!" I was told over and over again.

Well, I'm evidently severely mistaken in having responded to that term for the past 29 years. No doubt an oversight on my part, and that

1 **spanking new:** very new 23 **gasp** (n.): short intake of breath 25 **castigate sb.:** punish sb. severely · **brethren** (old use): brother 28–29 **be inundated with sth.:** be overwhelmed by sth.

of my entire family and reserve, not to mention the vast majority of the country.

While we were growing up we were all proud to be "Indians." The word had a certain power to it that set us aside from the white kids. (Or should I say children of occidental descent?)

Somehow the cry of "Proud to be Indigenous Population" just doesn't have the same ring.

Or picture this: You arrive thirsty in some new town, and you ask the first "skin" you see, "Yo, neeches, where's the nearest First Nations Bar?" Sorry – just doesn't work for me.

I guess at 29 I'm out of date. Oh, I understand the reasoning behind the hubbub. Columbus, as a member of the European Caucasian nation, thought he found India and so on.

That's cool, but there's also another school of thought that says Columbus was so impressed by the generosity and genuine nature of the Native population of the Caribbean that he wrote back to Spain saying these people were "of the body of God" – or, in Latin, "corpus in deo." *In deo* equals Indian. A pretty thin link, but who knows? I know some Indians with God-given bodies.

But a person in my position doesn't have time to defend himself with theoretical history. Since my *faux pas*, I've been too busy handling the deluge of politically correct terms I am permitted and urged to use.

It must be obvious to most people that in the past few years, Native people in Canada have gone through an enormous political metamorphosis, similar to that of people of African descent. Years ago they used to be called nigger, then Negro, then colored, then black and finally, today I believe the correct term is African-American or African-Canadian.

That's nothing compared to the selection of names and categories available to the original inhabitants of this country. And these names or classifications have nothing to do with any tribal affiliations – they're just generic names used to describe us "Indians."

Grab some aspirin and let me give you some examples.

We'll start with the basics: status, non-status, Métis. So far, painless. I guess next would come the already mentioned Indian, followed by Native, Aboriginal, Indigenous and First Nations. Pay attention, there's going to be a test afterward. From there we can go to "on-reserve", "off-reserve", urban, treaty.

12 **hubbub:** uproar 22 **deluge:** flood 25 **metamorphosis:** complete change 31 **affiliation:** blood relationship 32 **generic:** general

Got a headache yet? How about the enfranchised Indians, the Bill C-31 or reinstated people, the traditional Indians, the assimilated Indian? I'm not finished yet.

There are the wannabes (the white variety), the apples (the red variety), the half-breeds, mixed bloods and, of course, the ever-popular full bloods.

My personal favorites are what I call the Descartes Indians: "I think Indian, therefore I am Indian."

Get the picture? Right – there are a couple of dozen separate names for our people. Where does it all stop? I want to know just who keeps changing the rules.

Even I get confused sometimes. That's why I usually use the term Indian. I'm just too busy or too lazy to find out which way the political wind is blowing, or to delve deeply into the cultural/governmental background of whomever I'm talking or writing about. By the time I go through all the categories, I've missed my deadline. Then I become an unemployed Indian.

But I know what you're thinking. Why should I listen to this guy? What the hell does he know? He's probably just some status, off-reserve, urban, Native, Aboriginal, treaty, half-breed Indian. Well, this week, anyway.

(First appeared in The Globe and Mail, *April 16, 1992.)*

Powwows, They Are A' Changin'

When I was growing up, my mother used to tell me about how much things had changed on the Reserve since she was a kid. There were stories about hauling countless pails of water from the pump, chopping wood, fighting swarms of Indian-loving mosquitoes (without the benefit of OFF), wading through armpit-high snow to get to the outhouse while battling hungry wolves. You know, the usual.

When you're young, you don't listen, let alone conceive of life changing so much. But their stories have come back to haunt me. Because at the tender age of 31, I can't believe how much things have changed since I was a kid.

1 **enfranchise sb.:** give sb. political rights 5 **half-breed:** person with parents of different racial origins 26 **haul sth.:** pull sth. · **pail:** bucket 28 **OFF:** insect repellant 30 **conceive of sth.:** imagine sth.

Specifically, powwows.

When I was growing upon the Curve Lake Reserve, just north of Peterborough, Ont., the social event of the year was the annual powwow, which was held at (where else?) the baseball diamond. While some of my cousins and other relations would be dancing out their buckskinned little hearts, I'd be competing with the other kids to collect returnable pop bottles thrown away by tourists. Hey, it was a living.

Today, everybody drinks from cans, non-returnable cans. Sad, when the end of an era can be symbolized by an empty Coke can tossed into a garbage container.

Twenty years ago we thought it quite exotic when dancers from the Akwesasne Reserve, the Mohawk community near Cornwall, Ont., would come to dance at the powwow. We'd all stand around oohing and ahhing, pointing and whispering, "Wow, look, real live Mohawks."

Now, exotic has taken on new dimensions. I was recently at the Grand River Powwow near Brantford, Ont., where Native people from all over Canada and the U.S. showed up. There were even Native people from Central America dancing and selling things. A little more exotic than your average Mohawk to these now-jaded eyes.

In my youth, the majority of dancers wore ordinary buckskin with the odd colorful trapping – mostly beadwork and fur. If they were feeling particularly adventurous, they might wear white buckskin.

Today, the colors and designs are dazzling. Each of the fancy dancers – shawl dancers, grass dancers, jingle-dress dancers – and traditional dancers have a particular lifestyle. And you're lucky if you can find even a few wearing much buckskin, if any. Fashion trends have moved on.

Commercialism has reared its head, too. At some of the larger powwows, it is not uncommon to see prize money for the dancers and drummers in the tens of thousands of dollars.

It happens on a smaller scale, too. A few weeks ago I saw a group of tourists come up to two boys who were wearing dancing outfits. They marvelled at these kids for a moment, then asked if they could take their picture. Immediately, both boys, in stereo, stuck up two fingers and said in practiced tones: "Two bucks!" That's a long way from collecting pop bottles.

4 **baseball diamond:** baseball field 7 **pop:** fizzy drink 19 **jaded** (adj.): (here) cynical 21 **beadwork:** Perlenschmuck 24 **jingle-dress:** type of dress 27 **rear its head:** show itself 32 **marvel at sth.:** look at sb./sth. with astonishment

The food and crafts have also changed over the years. Long ago, all the money I made cashing in pop bottles was recycled directly into the powwow with the purchase of gawdawful amounts of traditional Native junk food: hamburgers, fried bread, corn soup and pop.

The menu of traditional Native foods offered at powwows has grown since then. It now includes pizza, candy floss, tacos, bologna on a scone and lemonade. At the powwow I recently attended, I saw two signs, side by side, one advertising buffalo burgers (made from real buffalo), the other peddling something called Indian burgers (I only hope it was made by real Indians, not from real Indians).

Other things sold at this powwow ranged from your basic tacky tourist stuff to expensive leatherworks, sculptures and paintings. There were several dozen booths, some with inventive names like Imagin-Nations and Creative Native, hawking standard Aboriginal paraphernalia like dream catchers, medicine wheels, glass beads, braids of sweetgrass, silver and turquoise.

Then there were the more … interesting items for sale. Playing cards designed in the style of one's favorite Canadian tribe. (I've got a full house – three Haida chiefs and two Cree medicine men. Beat that!) Another booth offered Tarot card readings, evidently a traditional Native activity I've not encountered before. At one powwow I saw a booth selling a large selection of New Age books. One publication in particular caught my eye: How to be a Shaman in Ten Easy Steps.

So, as I stood there in line waiting to use the portable Royal Bank money machine conveniently located beside the port-à-pots, I couldn't help but marvel at all the changes over the years. Powwows have gone high-tech and modern.

Then, off in the distance, I saw a man drain a bottle of pop and throw it away. It was one of the larger, still-returnable bottles. Feeling a twinge of nostalgia, I left the line, picked it up and put it in my bag.

Some traditions never die.

(First appeared in The Globe and Mail, *August 7, 1993.)*

3 **gawdawful = god awful:** great, huge 6 **candy floss:** Zuckerwatte 9 **peddle sth.:** sell sth. 11 **tacky:** cheap, in poor taste 14 **hawk sth.:** offer sth. for sale 14 **paraphernalia:** different things 29 **twinge** (n.): sudden short pain